Volume 1

O/A

EVERY DAY

30 day challenge

Know yourself
Love yourself
Be a better version of you

In general, about 1 out of every 6 adults will have depression, anxiety, stress at some time in their life. Depression, anxiety, stress, affects about 16 million American adults every year.

Anyone can get a mental problem, and depression, anxiety, stress can happen at any age and in any type of person.

Many people who experience depression, anxiety, stress also have other mental health conditions.

Stress, anxiety disorders often go hand in hand with depression.

People who have anxiety disorders struggle with intense and uncontrollable feelings of anxiety, fear, worry, and/or panic.

These feelings can interfere with daily activities and may last for a long time.

(CDC, WHO)

SHARE THIS BOOK TO OTHERS.
SAVE SOMEONE TODAY

Some people who are depressed may think about
hurting themselves or committing suicide
(taking their own life).
If you or someone you know is having
thoughts about hurting themselves or
committing suicide, please seek immediate help.

Call your mental health provider.
Get help from your primary doctor or other health care provider.
Reach out to a close friend or loved one.
Contact a spiritual leader, or someone else
in your faith community

This book is written to help you be a better person.
This is also written to save you from depression.

We know that everyone wants to reconstruct oneself
and start with a clean sheet but some people don't know-how.
That's why I write this book and tried it tested to help you recover
mentally and emotionally.
(This book saved me; I hope I can also help you
or someone you love.)

There's another book about moving on, but this is not it.
I suggest to finish this book before you read other volume to help you
recuperate.

Fixing yourself is one way to get your act together.
Concentrating on personal growth sets a good start.
Self-improvement, where there is
love, kindness, hope, and faith never go wrong.

Love yourself, before loving someone else.
Fix yourself, before fixing others.

Remember that ending your life will never be a solution.
Are you ready to restart the button?

After reading this book you will know
what is love and you will feel love.
You will know what the meaning of life is.
You will be a lot happier and be out of the woods.

Try to finish this challenge honestly.
Be willing to change
be willing to be better
be willing to heal!

Before you start this challenge write all your
worries, sadness, depression, fear, and anger in life.

_____
_____
_____
_____
_____
_____
_____
_____
_____
_____
_____
_____
_____
_____
_____
_____
_____
_____
_____
_____
_____
_____
_____
_____
_____
_____

After the challenge ripped this page and throw it away.
Look at it and read it one more time.
Say your goodbye and say that
"I will forget you and I will move on because
I love myself, my family, and the people around me."

Good morning!
Are you ready
to take the challenge?

You can read this every day at no specific time.
But, it will be more effective
if you will read this every morning.
To inspire you for the entire day!

REMEMBER
one page
at a time.

INHALE
EXHALE

(Repeat it 3x)

Before we start
you need to admit that no one is perfect.

All of us are making mistakes.

You are not always right.

Accept people's advice, learn to respect,
and learn to listen.

Not everyone wants to put you down.

Now is the time to turn over a new leaf
and bring the best out of you!

Hey, beautiful creature!
Wakey wakey!
Shake your body.
Relax your mind because
today will be a good day!

Turn to the next page for today!

You are worthy!

Keep that smile on your face.
It fits you!

Today's task is to
Prepare a good breakfast
for your family.

By the way,
you look amazing today!
Keep it up!

Turn to the next page.

Try to wake up early
have a 15 minutes' walk.

When you reached home say this
in front of a mirror

**"YOU ARE BEAUTIFUL
PERSON INSIDE AND OUT"**

Good morning!
Keep the blood pumping!

Release those beauty hormones.

Remember to sleep on time.
Drink hibiscus tea 30 minutes
before you sleep.

Because tomorrow is another day!

If God will spare you another day
be thankful and pray.
Because you have another chance
to be with your family and friends.

Share your blessing today!
Give food to someone you don't know.
Don't ask why?
Just do it.
Tell me what you feel after sharing food with others?

*(Write it on the last page of the book
and express yourself honestly.)*

It will make you feel
extraordinary.

Sharing is caring.

Challenge yourself today.
Show love,
firstly to your family.
Hug your parents and thank them.

Give them hugs and kisses.

Surprise your parents today!
Give them a present.

Drive somewhere far.
Listen to your favorite upbeat music,
It will help you boost happiness.

Think only **happy** thoughts!

*Listening to your favorite song
releases endorphins when stimulated
by loud music, so listening to **loud music**
is essentially self-medicating
once in a while .*

Try it! Have fun!

Practice seeing good in every
bad situation.
It will make your inner **beauty**
come out naturally.
You will never regret it.

No SODA day!
Drink only water and tea
to clean your body.
A healthy brain is in a healthy body.

Cheer up.
It's not the end of the world.
In everything you do,
make sure you choose
good decision.
Because good things
will never turn out bad.

Anxiety, stress, and sadness
can mess with your looks
and it will make you look grumpy.

Stay wrinkle free!

Forgive
someone today!
Even if it's not your mistake.

Try it!

I know it's difficult.

I feel you.

But you will feel like you release
a demon inside of you.
It will make you feel lighter.

*One of the hardest part of the challenge is to
forgive.
But forgiveness can help you move on
and live a happier, healthier life.*

Be **honest**.
Tell only the truth even if it will hurt.
Start changing from your innermost thoughts.
Your good aura will make your skin brighter.

By the way, don't forget to
drink 8-10 glasses of water!

No lies today.
Hate anything that is bad and continue doing things
that are good.

It's your cheat day today!
Eat something that will make
you smile.

Stay cheery!

It will give you **positive**
mind and energy.

Eat something healthy.

Kiss your grandparents
while your eyes are closed.

Thank them and hug them tight.

It's really hard to **accept**
and love your enemy.

But for your peace of mind, try it.

You'll feel better.

I swear.

If you're not yet ready, give yourself time.
Time to think and realize what
happened.

Acceptance is an active process.
It must be practiced.

Share a meal
to any homeless kid you will encounter.
Because sharing will bring out the best in you.
If you think that this is difficult to do.
Then you have a problem deep inside of you,
you need to learn how to share.

Always remember God loves a giver.

Let's fix you!

Trust me!
You'll feel great!

Show everyone who you really are,
by the way that you live.
Live in a good way.
Live in a way that brings peace, kindness,
and compassion to all people.
Try it.

One step at a time.

Get a post it.
Write
"You look great."
Or
"SMILE"

Add a smiley emoji
and give it to 10 person you'll see
who look sad today.

Share a smile
Because it's a therapy.
Help yourself by helping others
It's easy and free.

Are you confused?
Do you feel hopeless?
Do you feel tired?
You can't make up your mind?
Are you troubled?

There's only one solution.

Pray.

Remember that God is listening.
He knows what's deep inside your heart.
He knows what your tears are all about.

*Talk to HIM
and open up.
You'll feel better after you get a load off
your mind.*

MOVIE NIGHT
Surround yourself with good people.
Invite your friends over.
Watch a movie with your family and friends.

Create happy memories with your loved ones.
Spend time together will help you form a
stronger connection that will last a lifetime.

Don't cry.
Everything will be ok.
I know it's difficult.

Don't decide something when you're angry.
Be calm and grab some
iced coffee.

This is an icebreaker!
Sing your favorite song today!
Singing helps with blood circulation
that is good for your heart and mind.

Go to the beach.
Walk barefoot for 30 minutes,
while looking up at the sky.

*What matter is that you're taking steps
to improve your self.
Walking on the beach
helps your mental health.
Trust me!
I've been there.*

Always choose the good side
even if it will ruin your plan.

Again, good things will never turn out wrong.

So always choose good
and don't think twice.

Turn to the next page.

NO SOCIAL MEDIA DAY!

Today is your time for your 24 hours
social media cleanse.

Practice self-control.

Are you expecting a call today?
Or a message from someone?

Stop the waiting game.
You deserve something better.

If it's meant to be,
It will be.

Never force anything.
Trust the process.

Turn to the next page.

Don't be disappointed.

Something better is coming.

It's on the way.

Never rush things
and start believing.

Bake a cake today
and serve it to your family.

*Stop being lazy because
you need to be busy.*

Life is short.
Imagine it's your last day today.
What will you do to make your last day
memorable?

*Something that everyone will remember
and will make everyone proud of you.*

RELAX.
Take a deep breath.
Don't rush things,
you need time to think things through.

Call someone today and tell that person that

*"You're not alone. I'm here for you
because you are important to me."*

Think twice before you speak.

In everything you do,
put your HEART on it.

Divert your attention.
Clean your room and donate everything
you don't need.
Remember kindness will never be wasted.

A walk to remember.
Walk for 1 hour to release your
beautiful hormones.

*Walking for an hour reduces the risk
of major depression by 26%.
Keep walking.
Keep Moving.*

Turn to the next page.

Don't think too much.
Relax your mind.
If you feel alone, If you feel that no one understands you
always remember God is always there to listen.

He knows what's good for you.

Pray.

Have a conversation with your parents about your
future plan and what you're feeling right now.
Open up.

Not all fight is worth
fighting for.

Let it go.

Try choosing peace
and be a better person.

Debating, explaining or defending is the
same as fighting.
When you're fighting, your immune system will go crazy.
Your blood pressure will rise.
It will cause a lot of hairfall.

Look at yourself in the mirror
and say

"You can do it"

Stop making excuses
and
start making changes.

Do some cardio today!
Exercise to look and feel good.
Release those good hormones.
It will make you look healthier.

Go somewhere where you will
see the full night sky
and stargaze.

Did you know that stargazing will sharpen your eyesight?
and It's a stress reliever!
15 minutes of stargazing can help you feel refreshed.
which will help lower cortisol levels.

Lay down flat on the ground and look at the starry night.

Go to a park or somewhere
you will find a lot of people.
Say, "Hello"
to 5 strangers,
and smile at them.

This task will put smile on your face
while feeling the rush.
Start interacting with people genuinely.

Something fun!

Do you have a question that you can't answer?

If you do,
visit the nearest library or bookstore.
Get any book with the word **love** on the title page.

Turn it to page 11.
The first sentence is the answer to your question.

There is no scientific explanation for this.
I only want to divert your attention.
Stop thinking too much.
Give your mind a break.
Buy some chocolates.
:)

Release all the pain and the anger in your heart
because it will only cause lines on your face.
Anger will make your facial muscle stress.
It will give you more wrinkles and
you will look more depress.

Go out and buy a small cactus.
Or some pothos
or maranta plants
and put in on your coffee table.

Taking care of plants will help you
with your anxiety and depression.
It's proven to give you lasting effects of happiness.

Turn to the next page.

Don't let sadness eat you,
don't let sadness defeat you.

Don't worry.
Don't be scared.
God knows what's inside of your heart.
He knows why you're in pain.
He knows why you're crying in vain.

You are never alone!

.

Be good to all.
Reconnect to life.
Always pray.

Wear comfy clothes today.

Some Pj's and hoodies will do.

Go Infront of a mirror and say

"I can face this day with positivity because
I'm filled with love and hope"

*Looking at the mirror helps you shift your mindset
with authority.
Remind yourself how you improved.*

I'm happy for you!
Always show that beautiful smile.

Congratulations!

Thank you for completing this challenge.

I hope I was able to help you mentally and emotionally.

Always remember don't lose hope.
Have faith.
Stay kind.
Stay sincere.
Be honest.
Be peaceful.
Embrace love.
And share your blessings.

Because life is short to be wasted.

Keep running!
Never give up.

Because it's not over,
until it's over.

Write what you want to
change in your life

Write what you want to
improve in your life

Write what you want to
have in your life

Write your
future plan

Write your message here and give this to someone
who needs **emotional support**

This page is intentionally left blank for anything the reader wish to remember.

If you want another challenge get the
Every Day 30 days challenge volume 2.

If you want to move on after a heartbreak grab the
Moving On 30 days challenge volume 1.

If you want to be in good shape and look good grab the
Be You 30 days challenge volume 1.